BELWIN COMPLETE
ADULT KEYBOARD COURSE

A practical, enjoyable approach to learning to play all keyboard instruments

by Sandy Feldstein

Cover Photo: Stephen Simpson/FPG INTERNATIONAL CORP.

Editor: Debbie Cavalier

CONTENTS

Available Components for

THE BELWIN COMPLETE
ADULT KEYBOARD COURSE

The Method Book is a 96 page book with folk songs, popular music, classical titles and theory workbook pages.

The Accompaniment CD contains beautifully orchestrated and cleverly arranged tracks for exciting play-along performances. Each of the 44 selections are recorded twice on the CD; once with the piano and once without - allowing the student to be the star.

The MIDI ACCOMPANIMENT DISK contains the same fantastic orchestrations that are on the CD in standard MIDI file format. The MIDI disk provides students with the option of changing the pitch or tempo, assigning new sounds and manipulating any given arrangement to their liking.

The audio CD and MIDI disk have been prepared to enhance the student's practice and performace experiences. The 💾 icon located throughout the book the CD and MIDI disk track numbers for each of the 44 songs.

The Computer Software, available in both Windows and Macintosh formats, provides an interactive forum that helps reinforce the lessons throughout the book. Play music theory games and note reading games with immediate feedback from the computer.

4

THE PIANO KEYBOARD

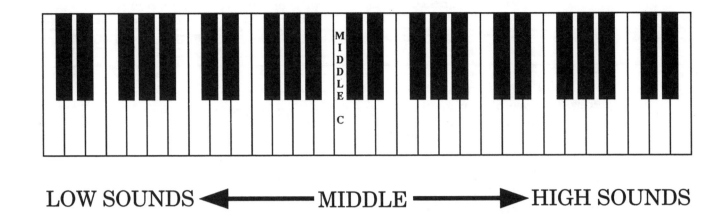

LOW SOUNDS ◄────── MIDDLE ──────► HIGH SOUNDS

RIGHT HAND and LEFT HAND
FINGER NUMBERS

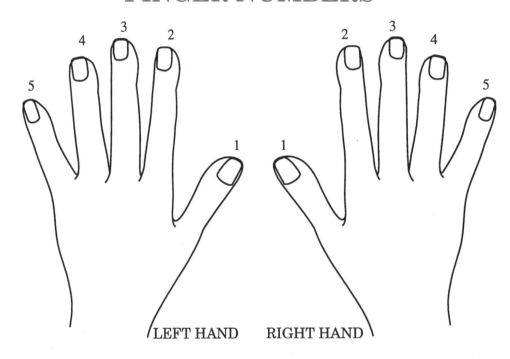

BLACK KEYS

The piano keyboard has black keys and white keys.

The black keys are divided into groups of two  and three.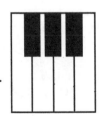

FINDING THE BLACK KEYS

On the keyboard below, circle each group of TWO BLACK KEYS.

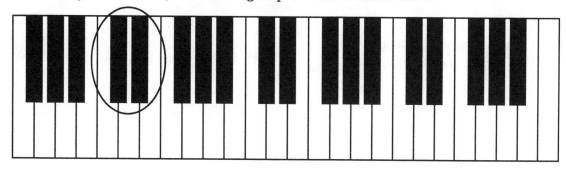

On the keyboard below, circle each group of THREE BLACK KEYS.

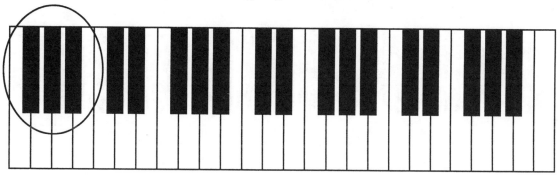

PLAYING THE BLACK KEYS

Left Hand

Right Hand

- Experiment by playing the groups of 2 black keys **from the middle of the keyboard down** (low sounds) with fingers 2 3 of your left hand.
- Experiment by playing the groups of 2 black keys **from the middle of the keyboard up** (high sounds) with fingers 2 3 of your right hand.

Left Hand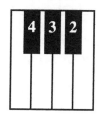

Right Hand

- Play the groups of 3 black keys **from the middle down** with fingers 2 3 4 of your left hand.
- Play the groups of 3 black keys **from the middle up** with fingers 2 3 4 of your right hand.

NAMING MUSIC NOTES

Music notes are named for the first seven letters of the alphabet, A-G.

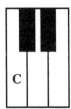

The note C is found
to the left (just below)
the group of 2 black keys.

The note F is found
to the left (just below)
the group of 3 black keys.

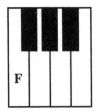

- Write the letter C on each C key. Remember, C is to the left of the 2-black-key groups.

- Write the letter F on each F key. Remember, F is to the left of the 3-black-key groups.

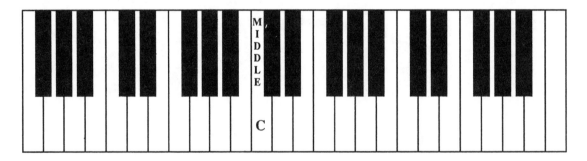

- Play each C and F on your keyboard. Play the ones below middle C with the 3rd finger of your left hand (LH) and the ones above middle C with the 3rd finger of your right hand (RH). *Note: a standard piano has 88 keys. Many of today's keyboards have fewer keys.*

- Using C and F as guideposts, you can find and name all the notes in the musical alphabet on the keyboard. The musical alphabet repeats A-G over and over. Now go back to the keyboard above and fill in the missing letter names. You've already done each C and F.

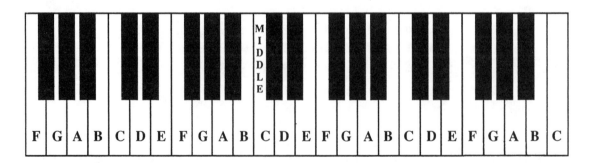

- Using any finger, play and name all the keys on your keyboard. Go up the musical alphabet from your lowest key to your highest. Play up to middle C with your LH and above middle C with your RH.

- Find and play the note A in each of its positions on the keyboard.

- Find and play each note in all their positions on the keyboard.

COUNTING RHYTHM

The duration of musical sounds (long or short) is indicated by different types of notes.

WHOLE NOTE   HALF NOTE   QUARTER NOTE

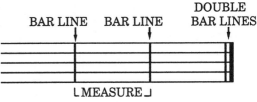

Music is divided into equal parts called MEASURES.
BAR LINES indicate the beginning and end of measures.
DOUBLE BAR LINES, one thin and one thick, show the end of a piece.

TIME SIGNATURES placed at the beginning of a piece of music show the number of beats
   (or counts) in each measure and the kind of note that receives one beat.

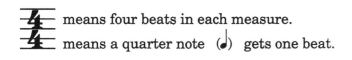 means four beats in each measure.

In $\frac{4}{4}$ time: a whole note o receives 4 beats
             a half note   receives 2 beats
             a quarter note   receives 1 beat

means a quarter note ( ) gets one beat.

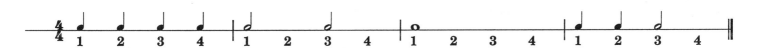

- Count with a steady beat while clapping or tapping the notes.
  Clap or tap once for each note.

RHYTHM REVIEW

Organized patterns of notes in time is called RHYTHM.

- Fill in the blanks.

In $\frac{4}{4}$ time:

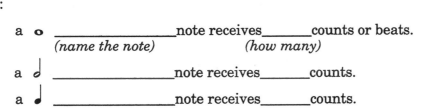

a o _____ note receives _____ counts or beats.
    (name the note)   *(how many)*

a _____ note receives _____ counts.

a _____ note receives _____ counts.

- Add the bar lines in the appropriate places. End with a double bar.

- Count and clap the rhythm.

PLAYING WITH YOUR RIGHT HAND

• Place your fingers over the keyboard and play each note.

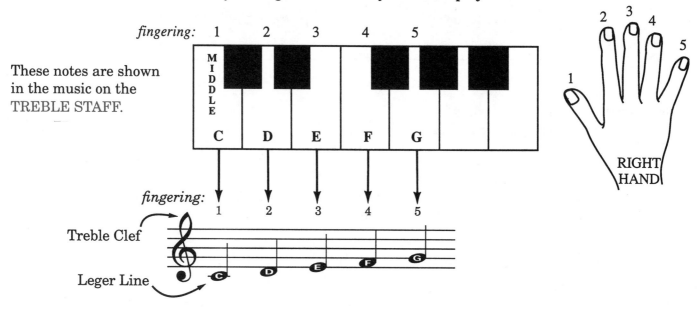

These notes are shown in the music on the TREBLE STAFF.

An extra line called a LEGER LINE can be added to the staff.
Middle C is written on the leger line just below the treble staff.
• Place your fingers over the keyboard.
• Play the music.

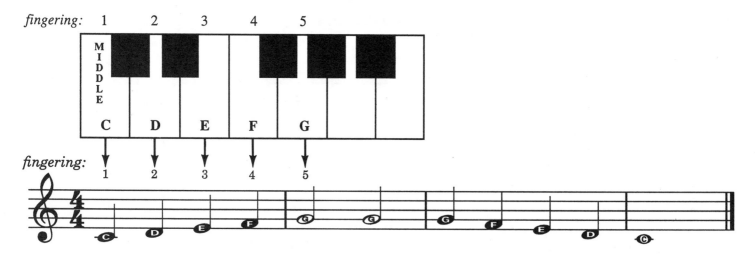

RIGHT HAND AEROBICS

The aerobic exercises will help limber your fingers.
Begin slowly, gradually increasing the speed.

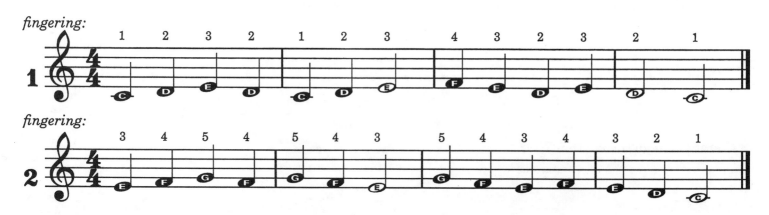

FAMILIAR MELODIES FOR THE RIGHT HAND

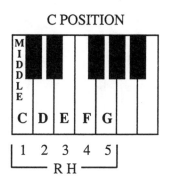

C POSITION

PRACTICE HINTS
- *Count 4 beats to each measure and clap or tap the rhythm evenly.*
- *Play the pieces while you count the beats.*
- *Play the pieces while you say the note names.*

MERRILY WE ROLL ALONG

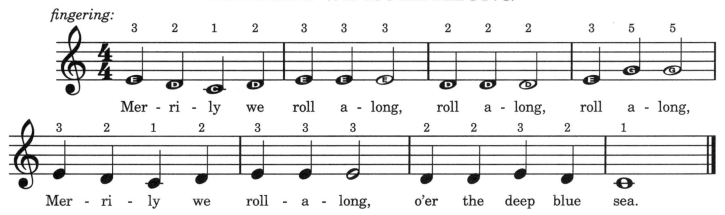

AURA LEE

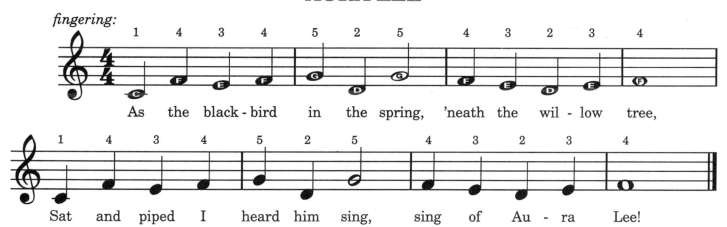

FOLK SONG

PLAYING WITH YOUR LEFT HAND

• Place your fingers over the keyboard and play each note.

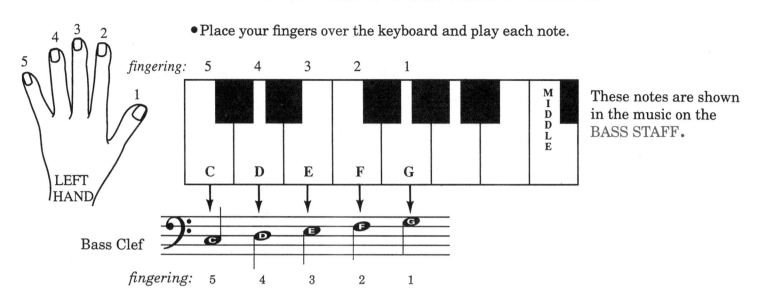

These notes are shown in the music on the BASS STAFF.

• Place your fingers over the keyboard.
• Play the music.

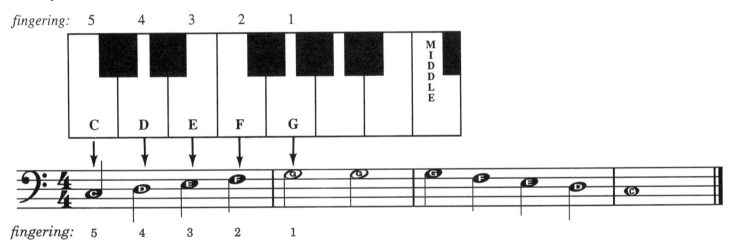

LEFT HAND AEROBICS

The aerobic exercises will help limber your fingers.
Begin slowly, gradually increasing speed.

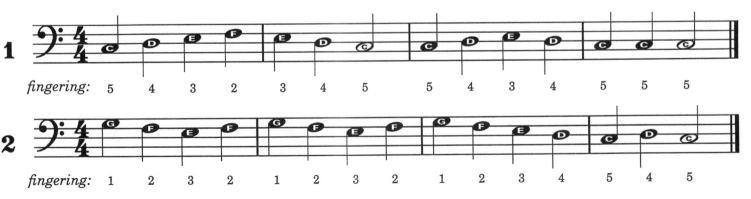

FAMILIAR MELODIES FOR THE LEFT HAND

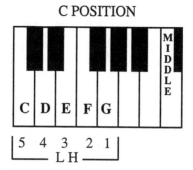

PRACTICE HINTS
- *Count 4 beats to each measure and clap or tap the rhythm evenly.*
- *Play the pieces while you count the beats.*
- *Play the pieces while you say the note names.*

ODE TO JOY

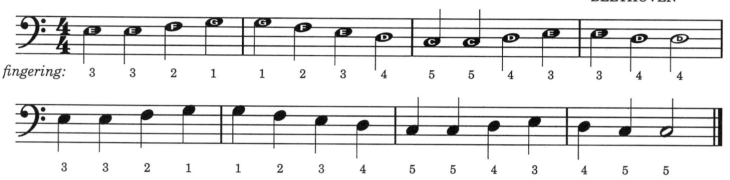

LIGHTLY ROW

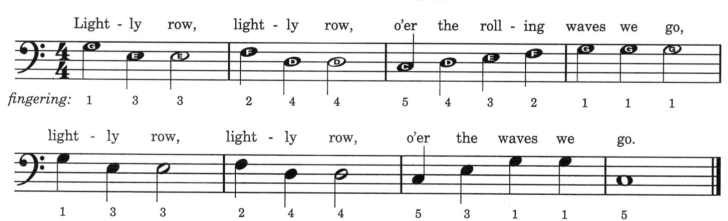

HOT CROSS BUNS

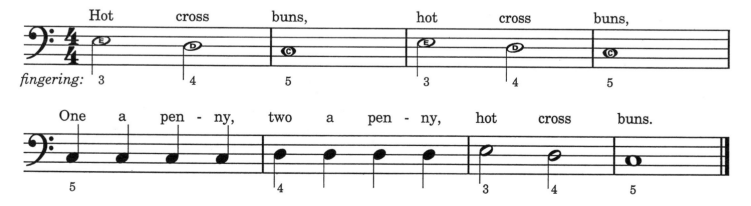

12

PLAYING WITH BOTH HANDS

• Place your fingers over the keyboard and play each note with each hand.
These notes are shown in the music on the GRAND STAFF.
The grand staff is made up of the treble and bass staffs.
They are joined together by a BRACE.

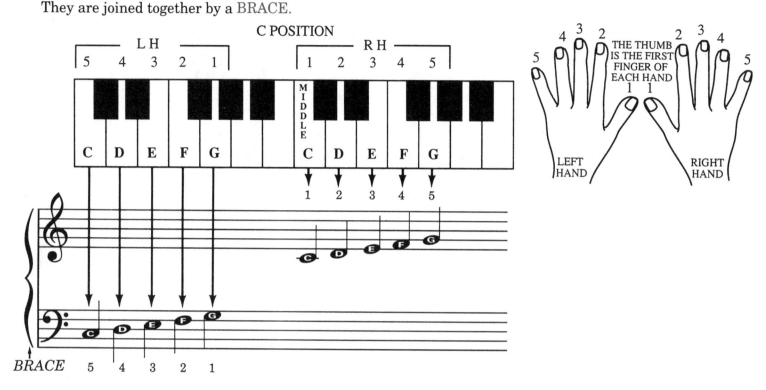

• Place your fingers over the keyboard.
• Play the music.

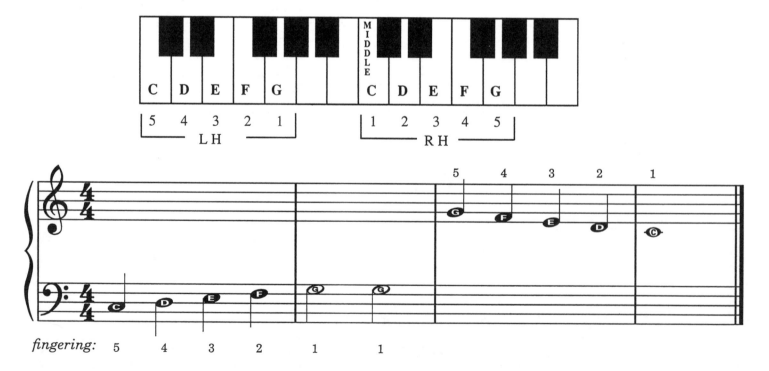

Keep both hands in playing position at all times.

FAMILIAR MELODIES FOR BOTH HANDS

PRACTICE HINTS
- *Count 4 beats to each measure and clap or tap the rhythm evenly.*
- *Play the pieces while you count the beats.*
- *Play the pieces while you say the note names.*

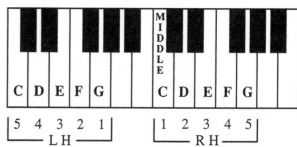

C POSITION

GOOD KING WENCESLAS

fingering:

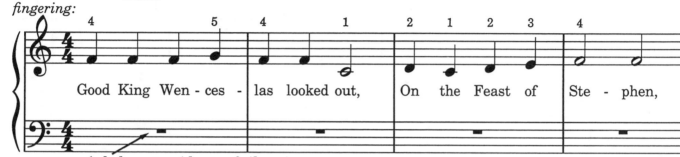

Good King Wen-ces-las looked out, On the Feast of Ste-phen,

(whole rest = 4 beats of silence)

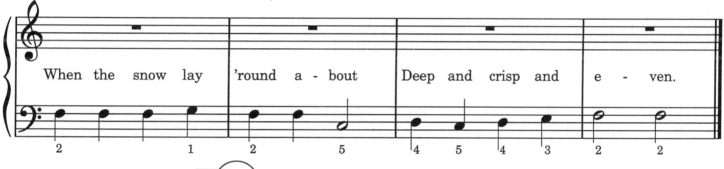

When the snow lay 'round a-bout Deep and crisp and e-ven.

LOVE SOMEBODY

Love some-bod-y 'deed I do! Love some-bod-y! Now guess who?

fingering: 5 3 1 4 3 2 5 3 1 2 3 4

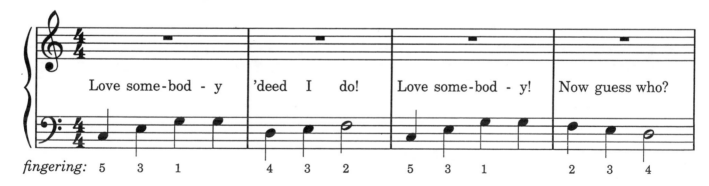

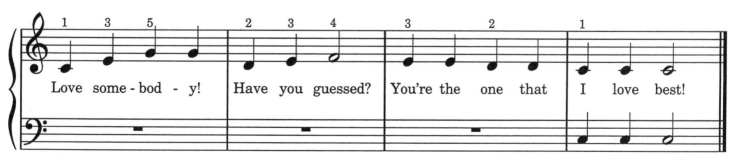

Love some-bod-y! Have you guessed? You're the one that I love best!

5

THEORY REVIEW

BOTH HANDS
C Position

The treble and the bass staff can be joined together by a BRACE which consists of a straight line and a curved line. The combined staffs are called THE GRAND STAFF.

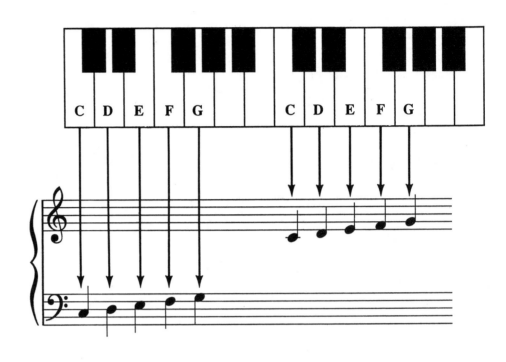

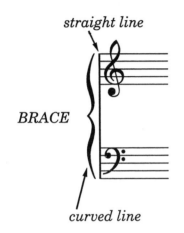

Name the notes.

Draw the notes indicated. Each note is shown twice.
Draw it once on the treble staff and once on the bass staff.

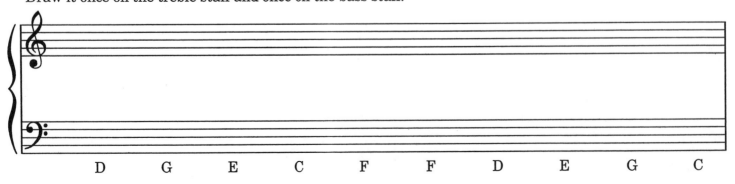

D   G   E   C   F   F   D   E   G   C

THEORY REVIEW

NOTES ON THE KEYBOARD
C Position

Connect the notes indicated
with the key on the keyboard.
Name the notes.

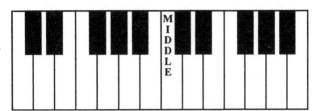

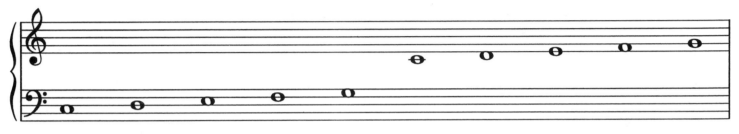

Draw the notes indicated
by the keys marked with an X.
Name the notes.

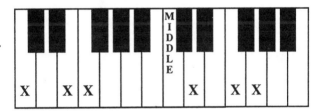

Write the letter names of the notes on the keyboard.

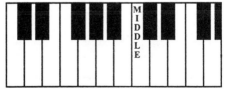

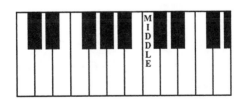

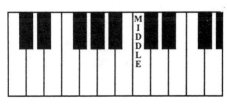

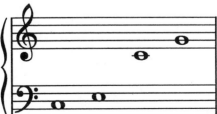

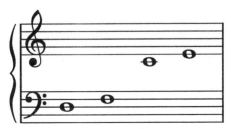

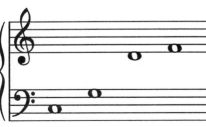

THEORY REVIEW

COUNTING RHYTHM

The duration of musical sounds (long or short) is indicated by different types of notes.

WHOLE NOTE — HALF NOTE — QUARTER NOTE

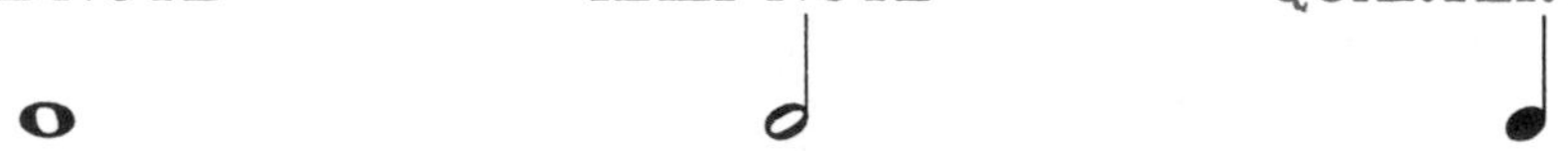

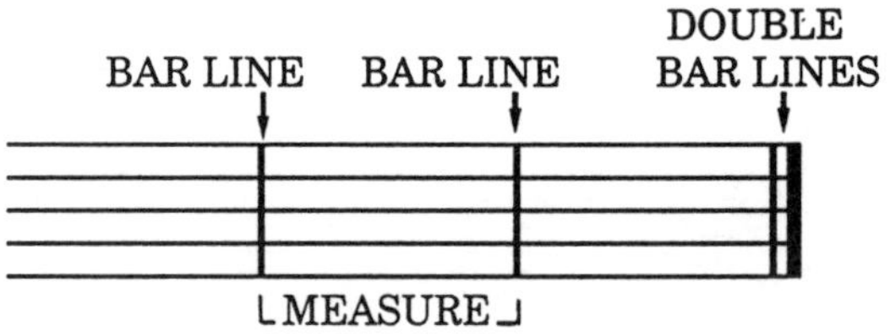

Music is divided into equal parts called MEASURES.
BAR LINES indicate the beginning and end of measures.
DOUBLE BAR LINES, one thin and one thick, show the end of a piece.

Divide the staff below into four measures and end it with a double bar.

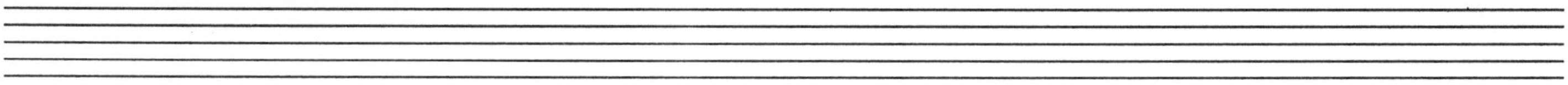

In 4/4 time a whole note receives four beats.

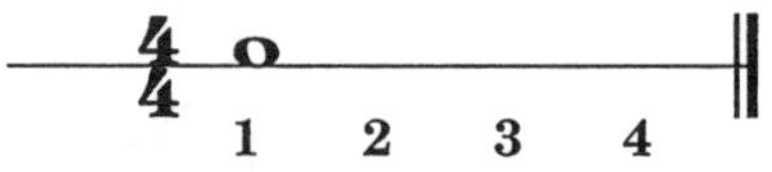

A half note receives two beats.

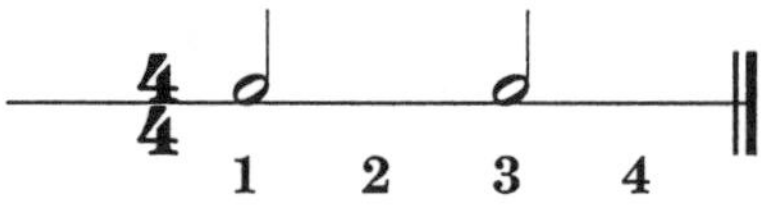

A quarter note receives one beat.

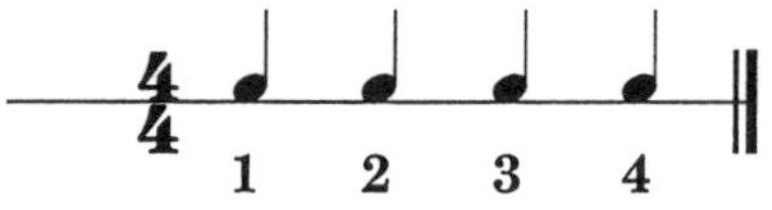

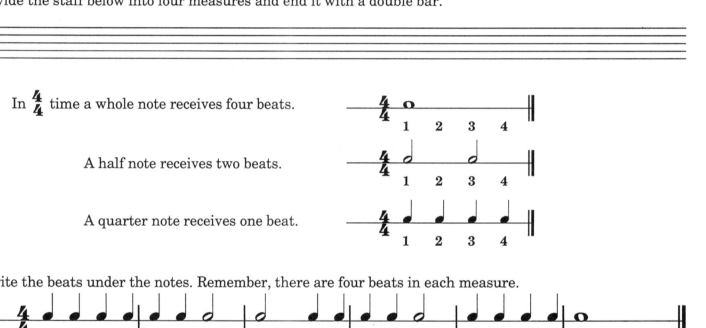

Write the beats under the notes. Remember, there are four beats in each measure.

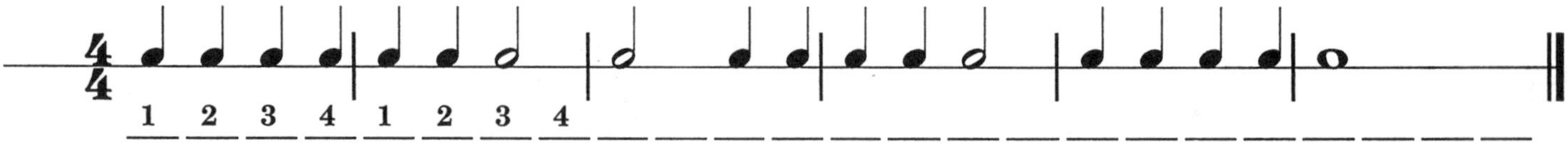

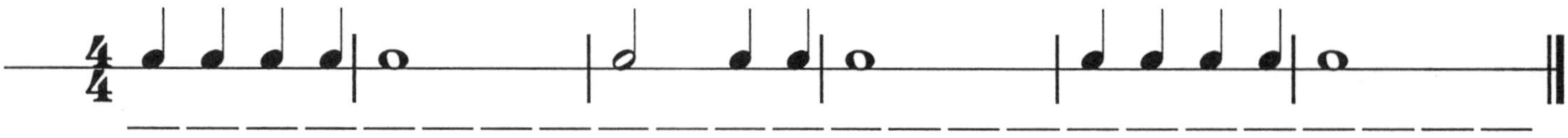

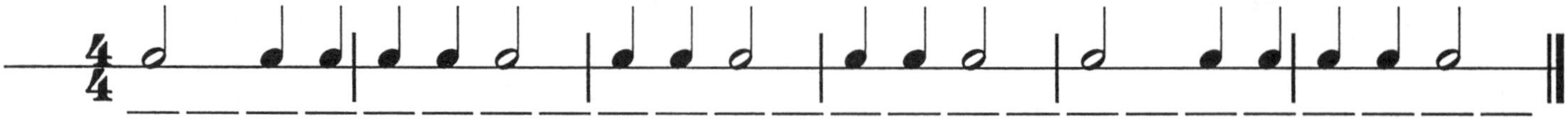

Add the bar lines in the appropriate places. End with a double bar.

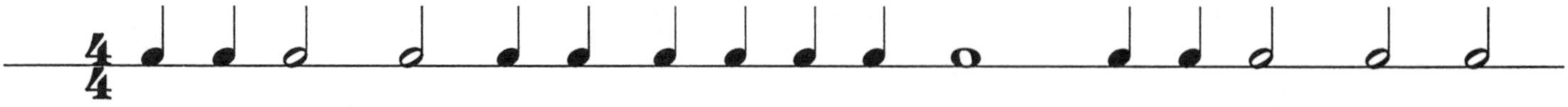

THEORY REVIEW

RESTS and TIES

The duration of musical silence is indicated by different types of rests.

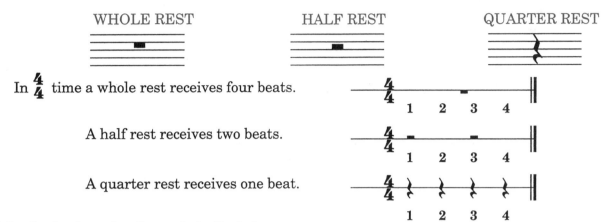

WHOLE REST HALF REST QUARTER REST

In **4/4** time a whole rest receives four beats.

A half rest receives two beats.

A quarter rest receives one beat.

Write the beats under the rests indicated.

Add the bar lines in the appropriate places. End with a double bar.

Fill in the missing beats with either rests or notes. Add only one rest or note in each measure.

NEW THEORY

A TIE is a curved line that connects two adjacent notes of the same pitch.
The tone is held as though the two notes are one.

Add the beats of the tied notes.

Draw the note that equals the number of beats of the tied notes.

PERFORMANCE TIME

C POSITION

THE TROLLEY SONG

Lyric by HUGH MARTIN
Music by RALPH BLANE

"Clang, clang, clang," went the trol - ley, _____

"Ding, ding, ding," went the bell, _____

"Zing, zing, zing," went my heart strings, _____ For the

(half rest = 2 beats of silence)

mo - ment I saw him I fell. _____

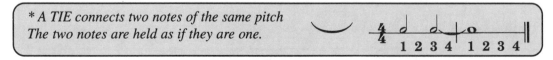

* A TIE connects two notes of the same pitch
The two notes are held as if they are one.

Not all music begins on the first beat of a measure. The beginning notes of the incomplete measure are called PICK-UP notes. The missing beats are frequently found in the last measure.

 ## WHEN THE SAINTS GO MARCHING IN

(pick-up notes)

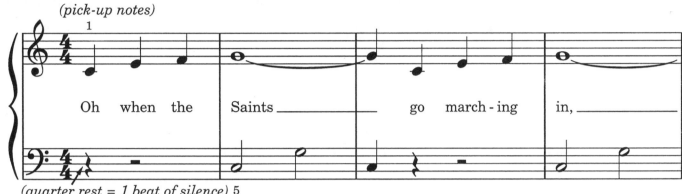

Oh when the Saints go march-ing in,

(quarter rest = 1 beat of silence) 5

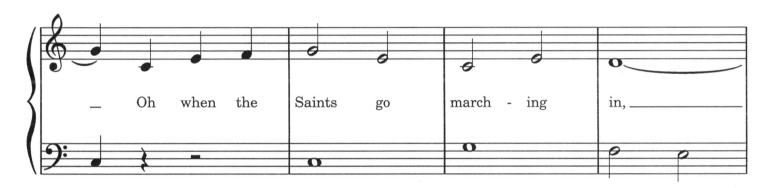

Oh when the Saints go march - ing in,

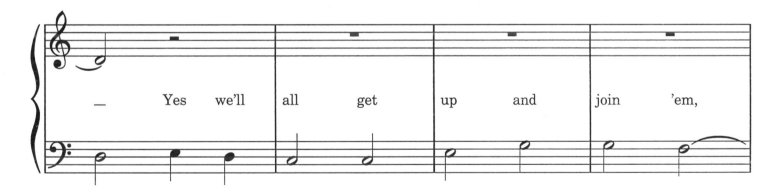

Yes we'll all get up and join 'em,

(missing beat)

When the Saints go march - ing in.

THE C CHORD

A CHORD is a combination of three or more tones sounded simultaneously.
The C chord is comprised of the notes C, E, G.
• Place your fingers over the keyboard and play each note with each hand.

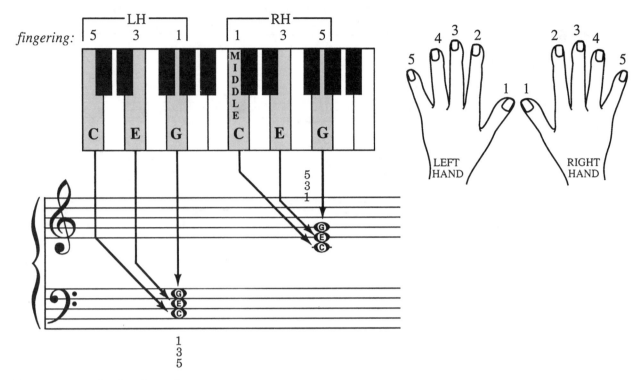

• Place your fingers over the keyboard.
• Play C chords with your LH.

• Place your fingers over the keyboard.
• Play the C chords with your RH.

• Place your fingers over the keyboard.
• Play the C chords with both hands.

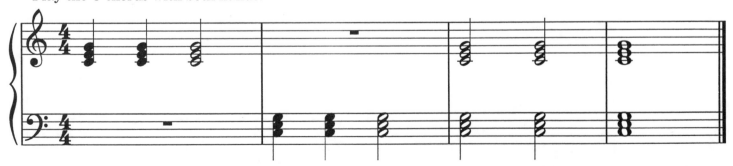

THE G⁷ CHORD

The G^7 chord introduces a new note, B.

The G^7 chord includes the notes B, F, G.

• Place your fingers over the keyboard and play each note with each hand.

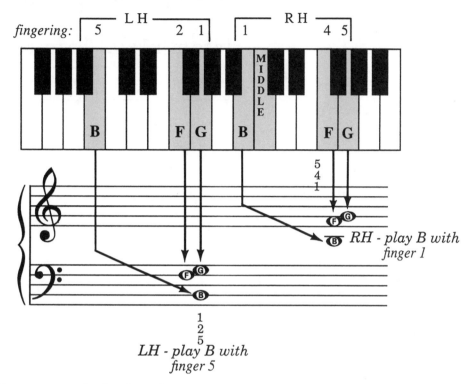

RH - play B with finger 1

LH - play B with finger 5

• Place your fingers over the keyboard.
• Play the G^7 chords with your LH.

• Place your fingers over the keyboard.
• Play the G^7 chords with your RH.

• Place your fingers over the keyboard.
• Play the G^7 chords with both hands.

COMBINING THE C AND G⁷ CHORDS

- Place your fingers over the keyboard.
- Play the C chord with your LH.

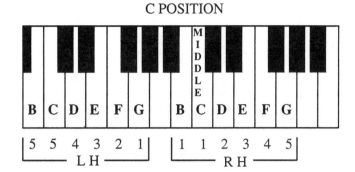

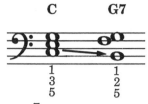

To play the G⁷ chord:
Finger 5 moves down one key from C to B.
Finger 2 plays F.
Finger 1 remains on G.

- Play the C and G⁷ chords with your LH.

CHORD SYMBOLS are indicated above the staff.

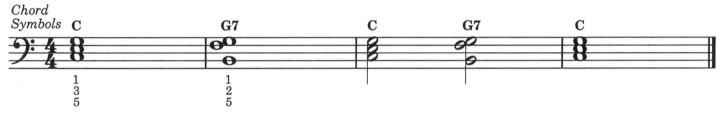

- Play the C chord with your RH.

To play the G⁷ chord:
Finger 1 moves down one key from C to B.
Finger 4 plays F.
Finger 5 remains on G.

- Play the C and G⁷ chords with your RH.

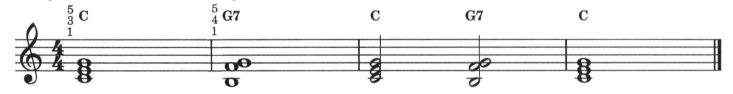

- Play the C and G⁷ chords with both hands.

FAMILIAR MELODIES
USING THE C AND G⁷ CHORDS

Practice RH and LH alone, then together.

LIGHTLY ROW

Light - ly row, light - ly row, O'er the shin - ing waves we go;

Smooth - ly glide, smooth - ly glide, On the si - lent tide.

MERRILY WE ROLL ALONG

Mer - ri - ly we roll a - long roll a - long roll a - long,

Mer - ri - ly we roll a - long, o'er the deep blue sea.

NEW NOTE B IN THE MELODY

You have played the note B in the G^7 Chord. Now you will play it in the melody.
• Place your fingers over the keyboard and play each note with each hand.

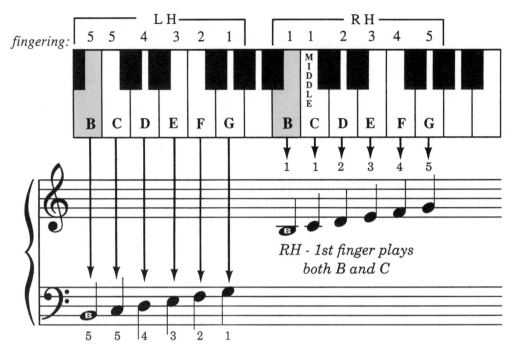

RH - 1st finger plays both B and C

LH - 5th finger plays both B and C

RIGHT HAND AEROBICS
with B

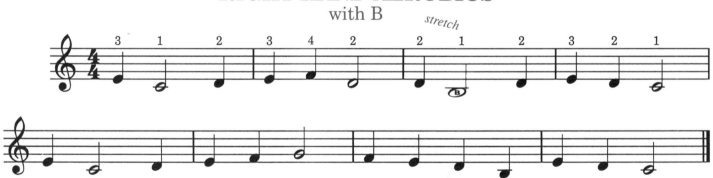

LEFT HAND AEROBICS
with B

USING B IN MELODY AND CHORDS

Practice RH and LH alone, then together.

MARY ANN

NEW NOTE A IN THE MELODY

• Place your fingers over the keyboard and play each note with each hand.

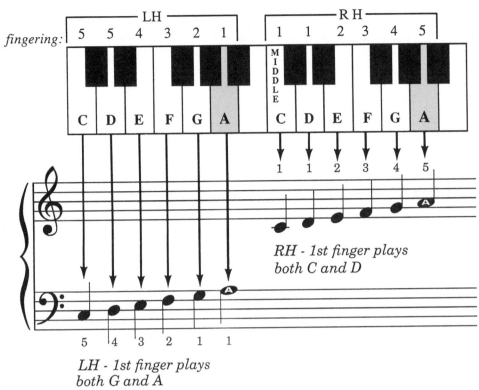

RH - 1st finger plays
both C and D

LH - 1st finger plays
both G and A

RIGHT HAND AEROBICS
with A

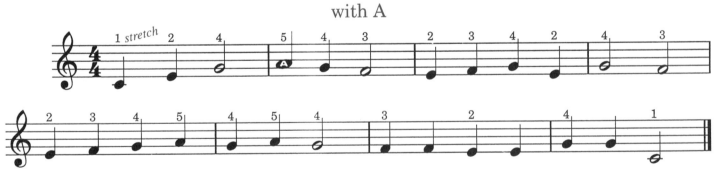

LEFT HAND AEROBICS
with A

C POSITION

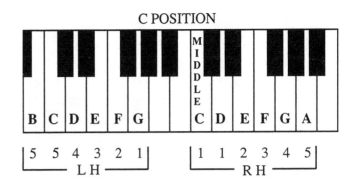

RH goes up to A, LH goes down to B.

A TISKET, A TASKET

THE F CHORD

The F chord uses the note you just learned, A.
• Place your fingers over the keyboard and play each note with each hand.

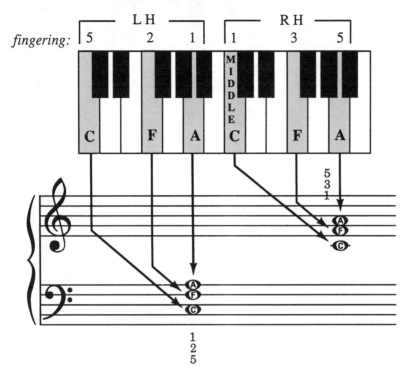

• Play the F chords with your LH.

• Play the F chords with your RH.

• Play the F chords with both hands.

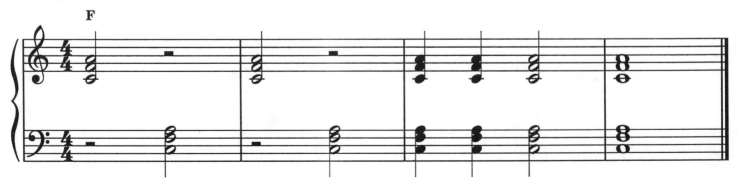

COMBINING THE C, F AND G⁷ CHORDS

- Place your fingers over the keyboard.
- Play the C chord with your LH.

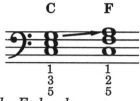

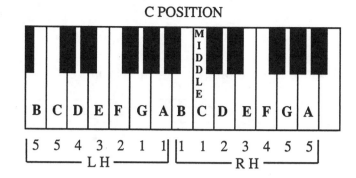

C POSITION

To play the F chord:
Finger 5 remains on C.
Finger 2 plays F.
Finger 1 moves up one key from G to A.

- Play the C, F and G⁷ chords with your LH.

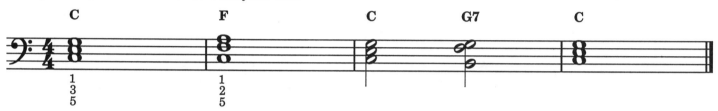

- Play the C chord with your RH.

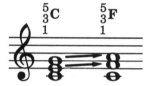

To play the F chord:
Finger 1 remains on C.
Finger 3 moves up one key from E to F.
Finger 5 moves up one key from G to A.

- Play the C, F and G⁷ chords with your RH.

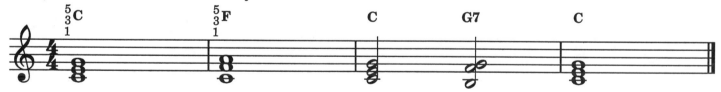

- Play the C, F and G⁷ chords with both hands.

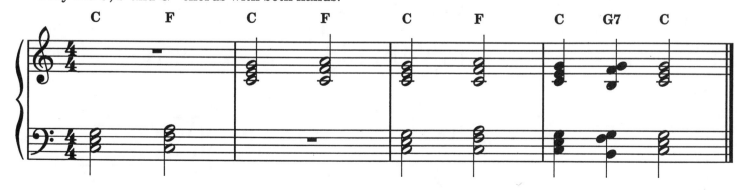

THEORY REVIEW
C and G⁷ CHORDS

A chord is a combination of three or more tones sounded simultaneously.

The C chord uses the notes C,E,G.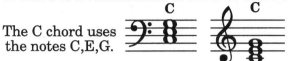

The G⁷ chord uses the notes G,B,D,F.

When playing the G⁷ chord at the piano, eliminate the D and move the G to the top of the chord to make it easier to play.

Name the chord.

Draw the notes of the chord.

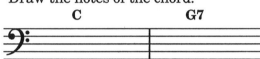 

Write the letter names of the notes of the chords on the keyboard.

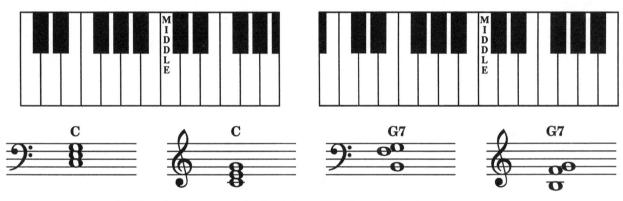

Draw the notes sounded by the keys marked with an X. Name the chord.

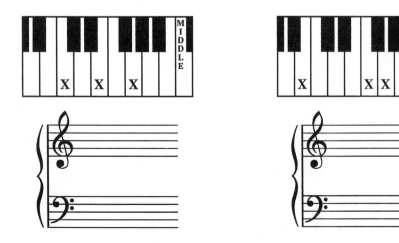 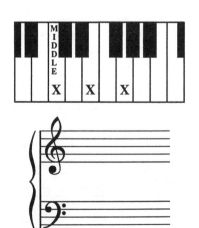

THEORY REVIEW
F CHORD

The F chord uses the notes F,A,C.

When playing the F chord at the piano, move the F and the A to the top of the chord to make it easier to play.

Name the chord.

Draw the notes of the chord.

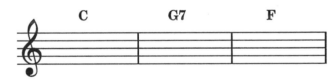

Write the letter names of the notes of the chords on the keyboard.

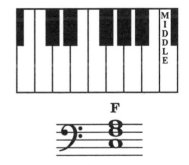

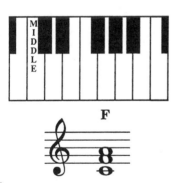

Draw the notes sounded by the keys marked with an X. Name the chord.

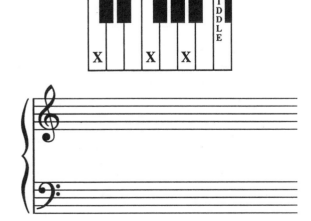

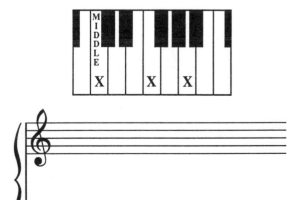

On page 19 you played THE SAINTS in a melodic fashion.
In this arrangement you add the C, F and G^7 chords.

Practice RH and LH alone, then together.

WHEN THE SAINTS GO MARCHING IN

The finger numbers will guide your RH movement.

THE VICTORS MARCH

LOVE SOMEBODY

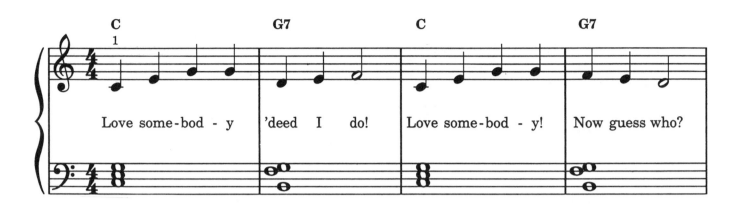

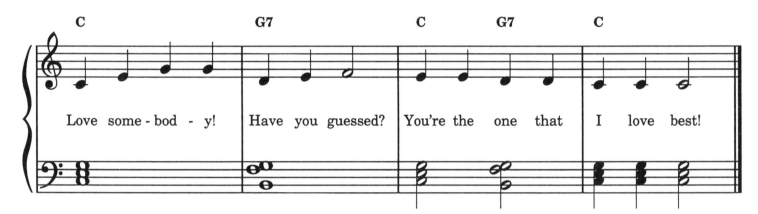

CAMPTOWN RACES

STEPHEN FOSTER

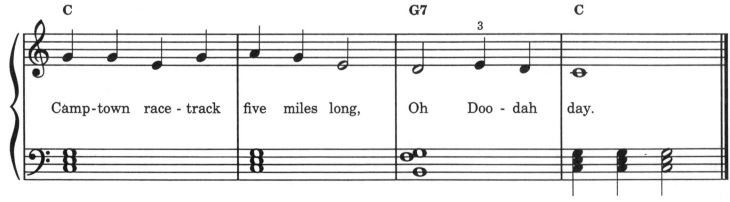

LONG, LONG AGO

T.H. BAYLY

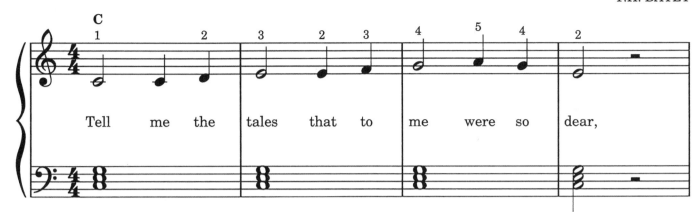

Tell me the tales that to me were so dear,

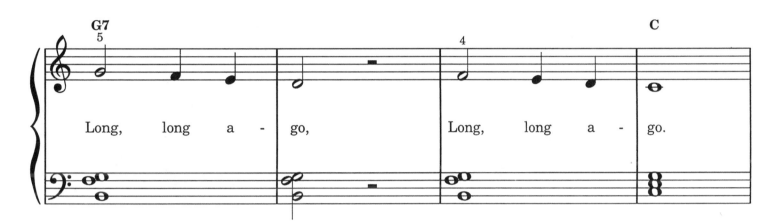

Long, long a - go, Long, long a - go.

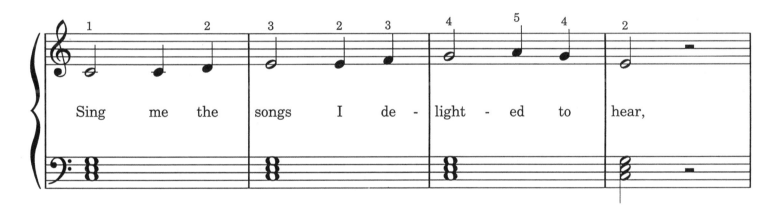

Sing me the songs I de - light - ed to hear,

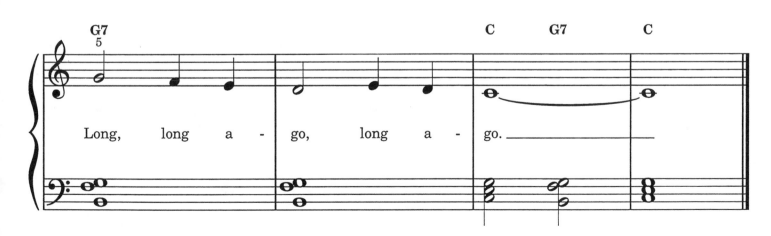

Long, long a - go, long a - go. _____

NEW TIME SIGNATURE

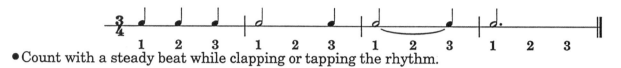

3/4 Time

3/4 means three beats in each measure.
means a quarter note gets one beat.

A DOT placed after a note adds one half the value of the original note.

A dotted half note ♩. equals 3 beats.

● Count with a steady beat while clapping or tapping the rhythm.

BEAUTIFUL BROWN EYES

The finger numbers will guide your hand movement.

FOR HE'S A JOLLY GOOD FELLOW

38

NEW RHYTHM

An eighth note ♪ receives 1/2 a beat.

Two eighth notes ♫ equal 1 quarter note. ♫ = ♩
1 & = 1 &

Count with a steady beat while clapping or tapping the rhythm.
(Count "1 and 2 and 3 and 4 and.")

FAMILIAR MELODIES USING EIGHTH NOTES

BAA, BAA BLACK SHEEP

Baa, baa black sheep have you an - y wool?   Yes sir, yes sir, three bags full.

I'M IN THE MOOD FOR LOVE

I'm in the mood for love,

OVER THE RAINBOW

Some-where   O - ver The Rain-bow,

THIS OLD MAN

This old man,   he played one,   He played nick-nack   on   my   thumb, With a

nick-nack pad-dy whack, give the dog a bone!   This old man came roll - ing home.

DYNAMIC SIGNS tell you how loud or soft to play.
f = Forte and means to play loud.
p = Piano and means to play soft.

The finger numbers will guide your hand movement.

THIS OLD MAN

THEORY REVIEW

EIGHTH NOTES

One eighth note looks like a quarter note with a flag added to its stem.

Groups of two or four eighth notes are joined by a beam.

Two eighth notes equal one quarter note.

Four eighth notes equal one half note.

Eight eighth notes equal one whole note.

In $\frac{4}{4}$ time an eighth note receives 1/2 a beat.

Write the beats under the notes.

Add the bar lines in the appropriate places. End with a double bar.

Fill in the missing beats with either rests or notes.

Add the beats of the notes indicated.

Draw the note that equals the number of beats

DYNAMIC SIGNS tell you how loud or soft to play the music.

f = *Forte* and means to play loud.

p = *Piano* and means to play soft.

Draw the symbol that indicates the volume level.

soft _____   loud _____

MUSETTE
(Theme)

J.S. BACH
arr. by S. Feldstein

 # ROCK ON DOWN

Moderate rock feel

by S. FELDSTEIN

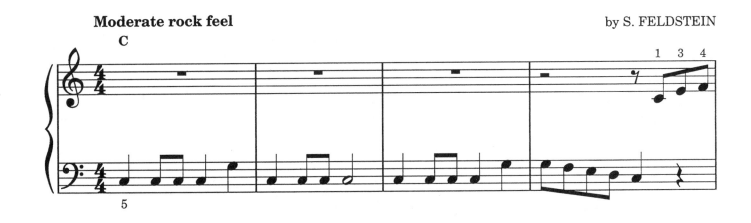

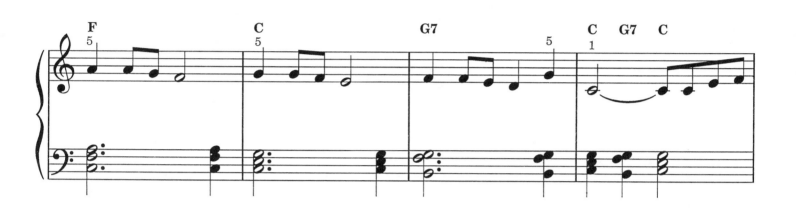

NEW POSITION
MIDDLE C

In the Middle C position both thumbs are on C.
• Place your fingers over the keyboard and play each note with each hand.

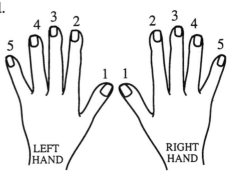

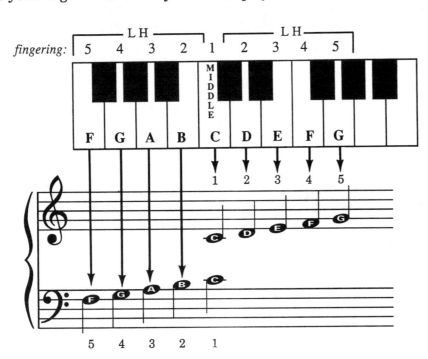

In the Middle C position you can play many new melodies.

THEME FROM SYMPHONY No. 1

Brahms

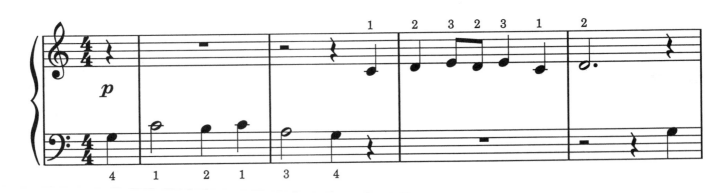

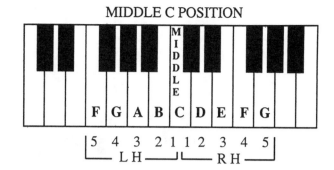

MIDDLE C POSITION

IT AIN'T GONNA RAIN NO MORE

It ain't gon-na rain, it ain't gon-na snow, It ain't gon-na rain no more;

Come on ev'-ry bod-y now, It ain't gon-na rain no more; It

ain't gon-na rain, it ain't gon-na snow, It ain't gon-na rain no more;

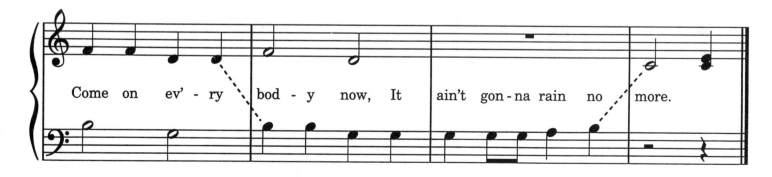

Come on ev'-ry bod-y now, It ain't gon-na rain no more.

THEORY REVIEW
MIDDLE C POSITION

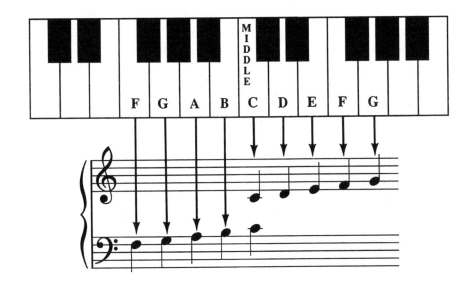

Name the notes indicated.

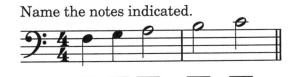

Draw the notes indicated.

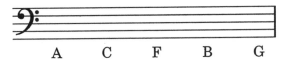

A   C   F   B   G

Draw the notes sounded by the keys marked with an X.

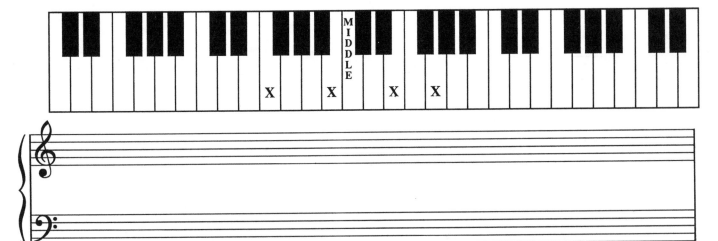

Write the letter names of the notes on the keyboard.

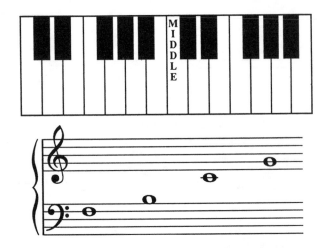

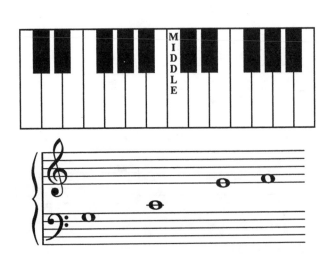

DANCE OF THE SLAVE MAIDENS
Middle C Position

A. BORODIN
arr. by S. Feldstein

47

48

Count:

4 & 1 & 2 & 3 & 4 &

stems down = LH
stems up = RH

SINGIN' IN THE RAIN
Middle C Position

22 ⊕ 66

Words by ARTHUR FREED
Music by NACIO HERB BROWN

f I'm Sing - in' In The Rain, Just Sing - in' In The Rain. What a

glo - ri - ous feel - ing, I'm hap - py a - gain, I'm

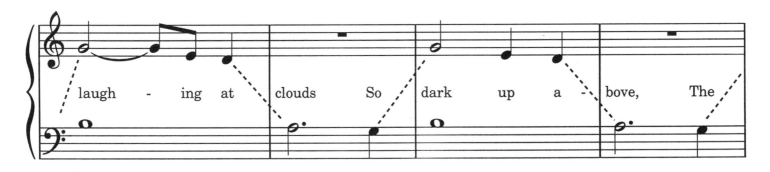

laugh - ing at clouds So dark up a - bove, The

sun's ___ in my heart And I'm rea - dy for love. Let the

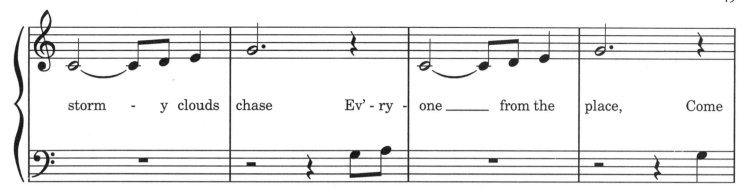

storm - y clouds chase   Ev' - ry - one _____ from the   place,   Come

on _____ with the   rain,   I've a   smile _____ on my   face.   I'll

walk   down the   lane   with a   hap - py re - frain,   And

sing - in' just   Sing - in' In The   Rain.

WE THREE KINGS OF ORIENT ARE
Middle C Position

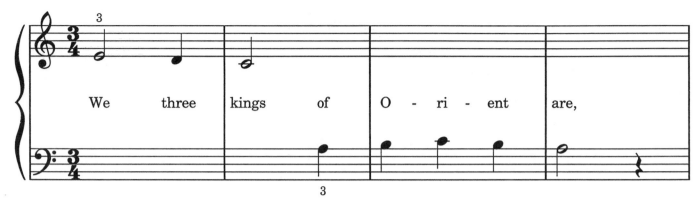

We three kings of O - ri - ent are,

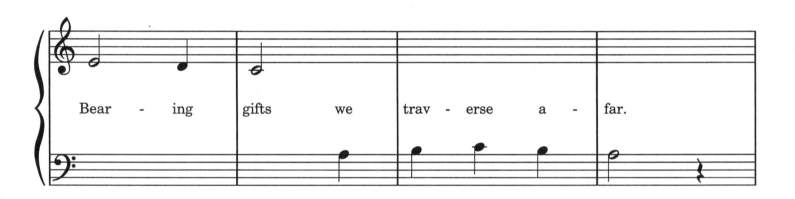

Bear - ing gifts we trav - erse a - far.

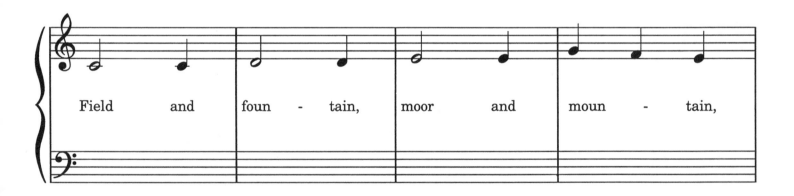

Field and foun - tain, moor and moun - tain,

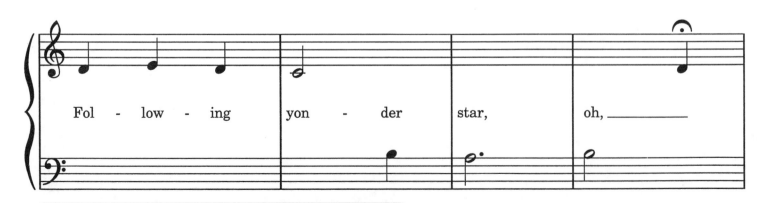

Fol - low - ing yon - der star, oh, _____

= fermata or hold. Hold the note longer than indicated.

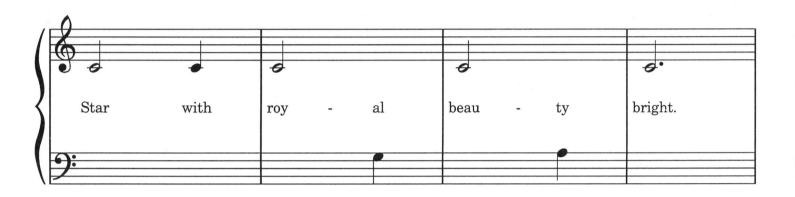

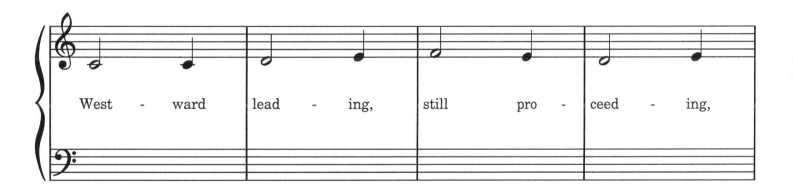

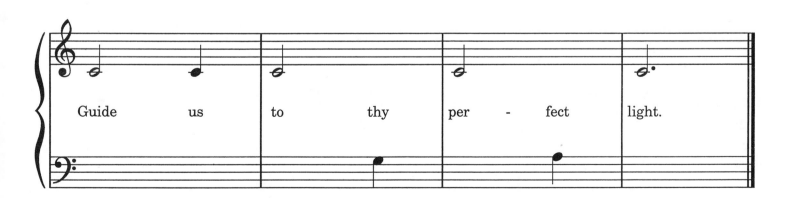

LIEBESTRAUM

Middle C Position

FRANZ LISZT
arr. by S. Feldstein

Moderately, in a singing style

Franz Liszt
(1811-1886)

CHORD ACCOMPANIMENTS

Now that you've played some songs in the middle C position, let's return to the original C position
so you can have some more fun with chords.

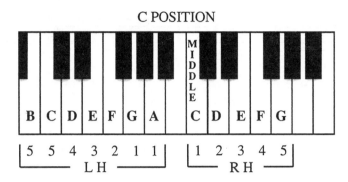

- Place both hands in the C position.

Instead of playing all the notes of the LH chord together,
play the lowest note first (alone) and then play the
other notes of the chord together.

- Play the C and G⁷ chord accompaniment pattern.

This is how the last 8 measures of THE VICTORS MARCH sounds with
the accompaniment pattern. Compare it to the arrangement on page 27.

Practice RH and LH alone, then together.
The finger numbers will guide your hand movement.

THE CAISSONS GO ROLLING ALONG

EDMUND GRUBER

You can now go back to all the songs in $\frac{4}{4}$ time that you have played that have chords in the LH and play them using the accompaniment pattern.
Page 23: LIGHTLY ROW; MERRILY WE ROLL ALONG   page 25: MARY ANN
Page 32: WHEN THE SAINTS GO MARCHING IN   page 33: THE VICTORS MARCH
Page 39: THIS OLD MAN

CHORD ACCOMPANIMENT IN $\frac{3}{4}$ TIME

The same style accompaniment pattern also sounds great in $\frac{3}{4}$ time.

In measures 1 and 9, the 1st note of the melody is played by the 1st finger of the LH.

DOWN IN THE VALLEY

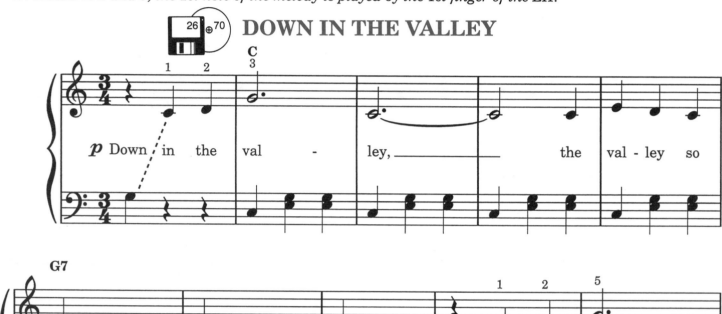

You can now go back to the $\frac{3}{4}$ songs that you have played that have chords in the LH and play them using the accompaniment pattern.

page 36: BEAUTIFUL BROWN EYES   page 37: FOR HE'S A JOLLY GOOD FELLOW

Here is another 4/4 *song.*

POLLY WOLLY DOODLE

CARNIVAL OF VENICE

J. BENEDICT
arr. by S. Feldstein

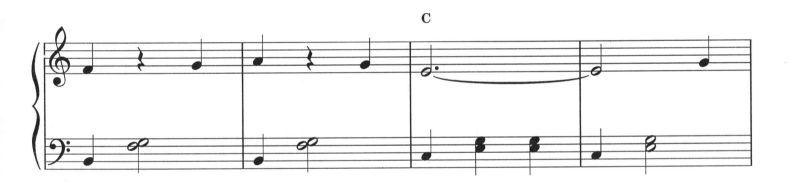

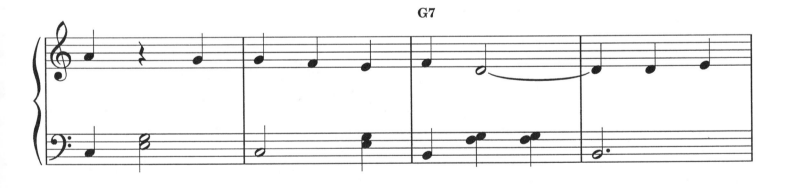

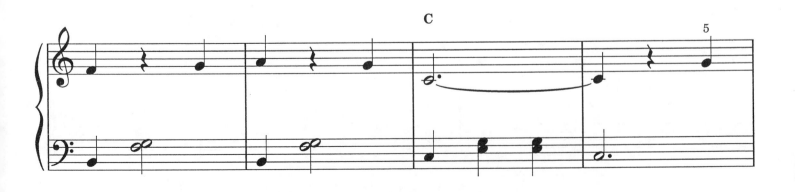

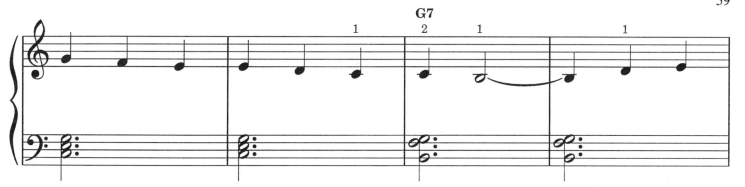

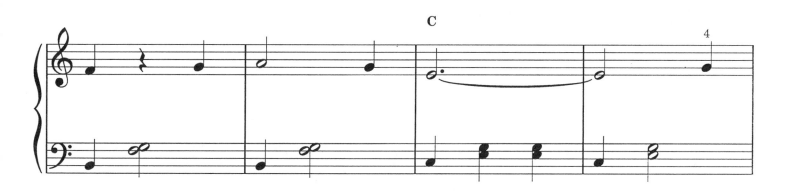

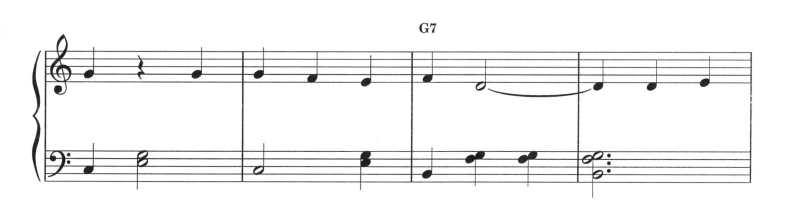

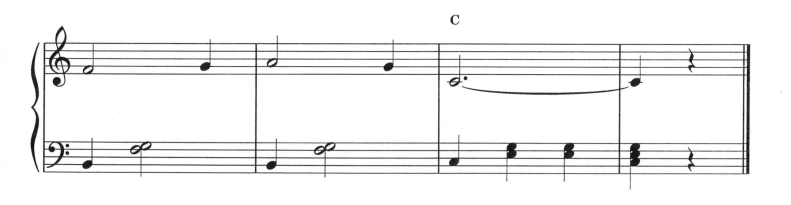

WALTZ FOR WENDY

Moderate

by S. FELDSTEIN

NEW NOTE
F♯ (F sharp)

• Place your fingers over the keyboard and play each note with each hand.

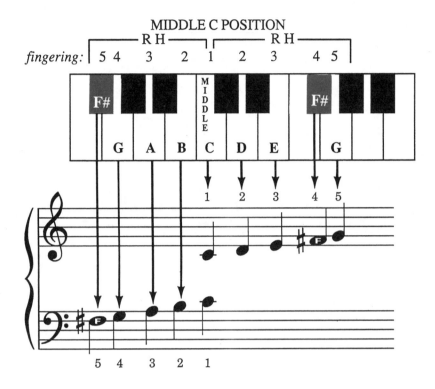

F♯ (F sharp) is the black key to the right of *(higher than)* F.

F♯ AEROBICS
(based on "Chester")

KEY SIGNATURE

When the F# is indicated at the beginning of the piece of music, it means every F in the piece is played F#

MIDDLE C POSITION

SWEET MARIE

R. MOORE

Come to me, Sweet Ma - rie, Sweet Ma - rie, come to me, Not be -
-cause your face is fair, love to see._____ But your
soul so pure and sweet, Makes my hap - pi - ness com - plete, Makes me
fal - ter at your feet, Sweet Ma - rie._____

THEORY REVIEW

SHARPS

When you look at the piano keyboard, the black key to the right of each white key has the same note name with the addition of a sharp.

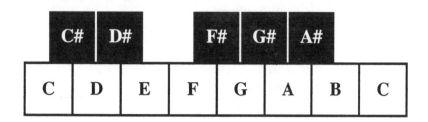

F♯ (F sharp) is the black key to the right of (higher than) F.

Name the notes indicated.

_____ _____ _____ _____ _____   _____ _____ _____ _____

Draw the notes indicated.

B   F♯   A   A   F♯   B

KEY SIGNATURE

When the F♯ is indicated at the beginning of the piece of music, it means every F in the piece is played F♯.

Draw the notes sounded by the keys marked with an X.

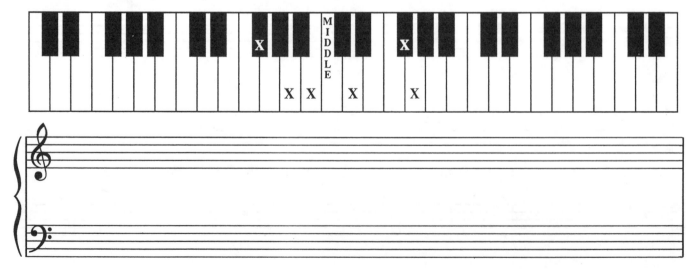

FINALE
from Quartet in F
Middle C Position

J. HAYDN
arr. by S. Feldstein

THEME FROM ICE CASTLES
(Through the Eyes of Love)

by CAROLE BAYER SAGER
and MARVIN HAMLISCH
arr. by S. Feldstein

Moderate

Please don't let this feel - ing end, it's ev - 'ry - thing I

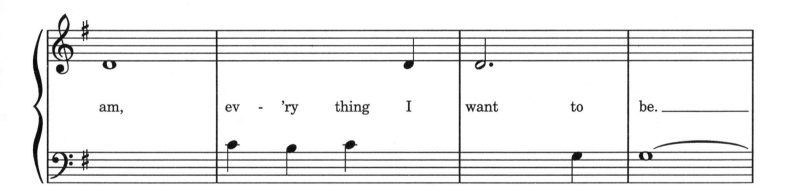

am, ev - 'ry thing I want to be. ____

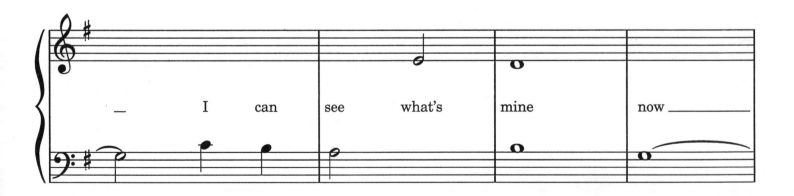

___ I can see what's mine now ____

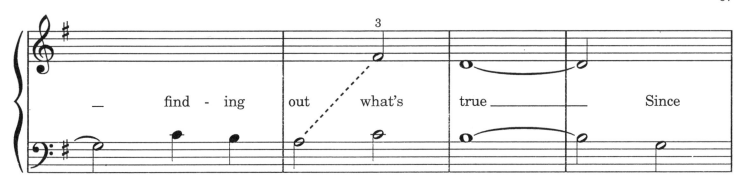

_ find - ing out what's true _____ Since

I found you _____ look - ing

through the eyes _____ of love. _____

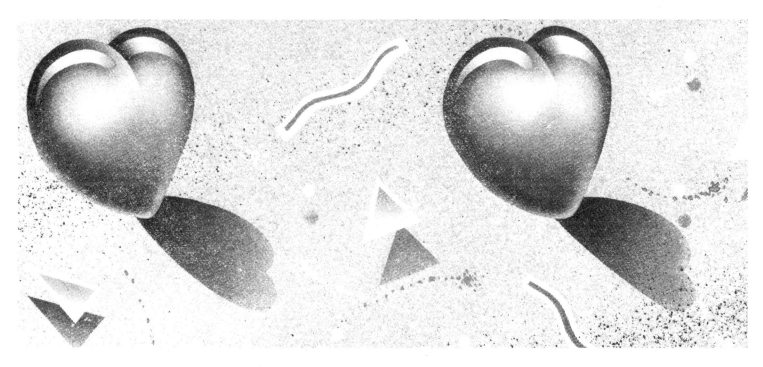

NEW POSITION
G POSITION

• Place your fingers over the keyboard and play each note with each hand.

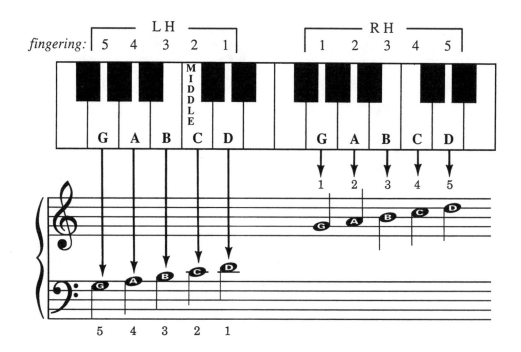

WALTZ IN G

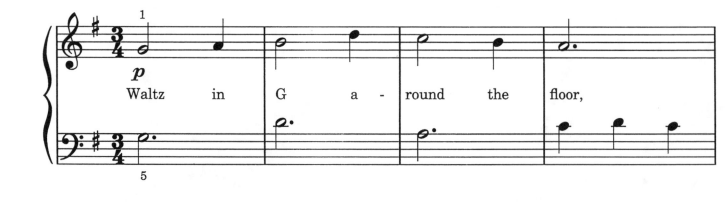

Waltz in G a - round the floor,

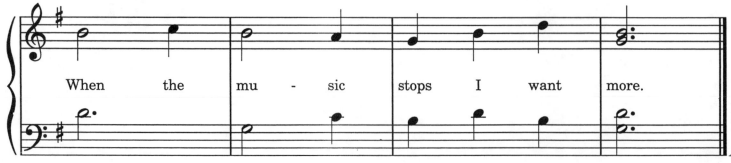

When the mu - sic stops I want more.

THE G CHORD

The G chord is comprised of the notes G, B, D.
* Place your fingers over the keyboard and play each note with each hand.

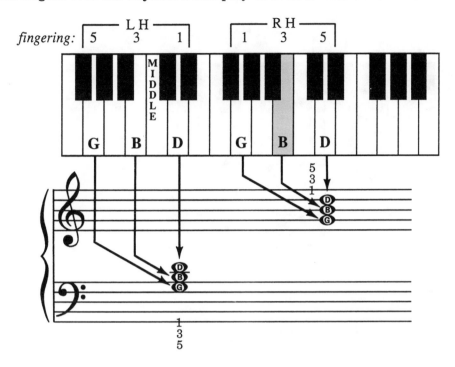

* Play the G chords with your LH.

* Play the G chords with your RH.

* Play the G chords with both hands.

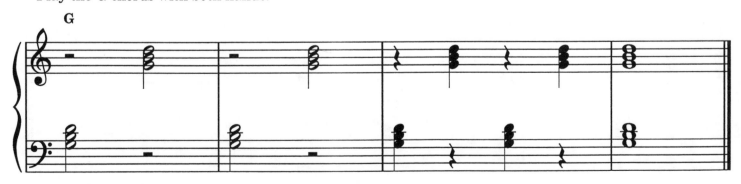

THE D^7 CHORD

The D^7 chord includes the notes F♯, C, D.
• Place your fingers over the keyboard and play each note with each hand.

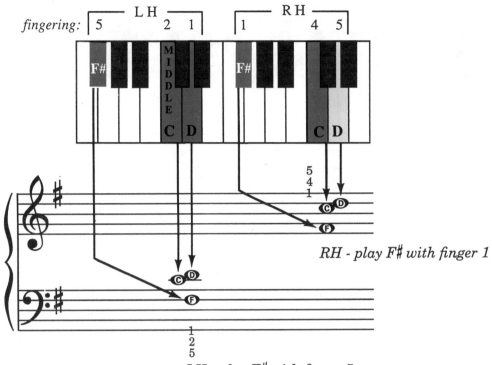

RH - play F♯ with finger 1

LH - play F♯ with finger 5

• Play the D^7 chords with your LH.

• Play the D^7 chords with your RH.

• Play the D^7 chords with both hands.

COMBINING THE G AND D⁷ CHORDS

•Play the G chord with your LH.

G POSITION

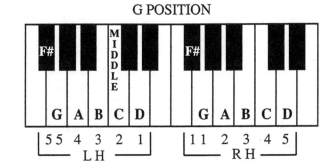

To play the D⁷ chord:
  Finger 5 moves down one key from G to F♯.
  Finger 2 plays C.
  Finger 1 remains on D.

•Play the G and D⁷ chords with your LH.

•Play the G chord with your RH.

To play the D⁷ chord:
  Finger 1 moves down one key from G to F♯.
  Finger 4 plays C.
  Finger 5 remains on D.

•Play the G and D⁷ chords with your RH.

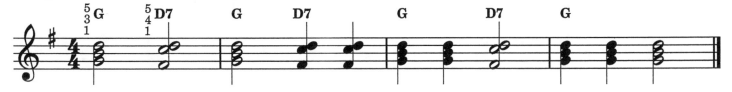

•Play the G and D⁷ chords with both hands.

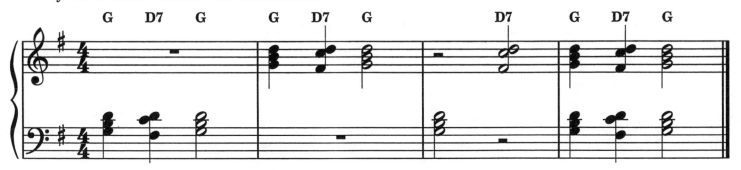

FAMILIAR MELODY USING THE G AND D⁷ CHORDS

NEW NOTE E IN THE MELODY

• Place your fingers over the keyboard and play each note with each hand.

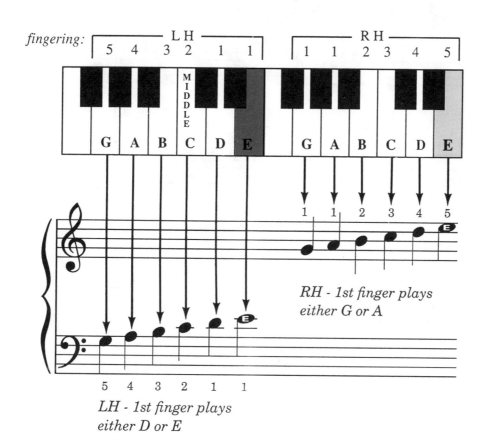

RH - 1st finger plays either G or A

LH - 1st finger plays either D or E

RIGHT HAND AEROBICS
with E

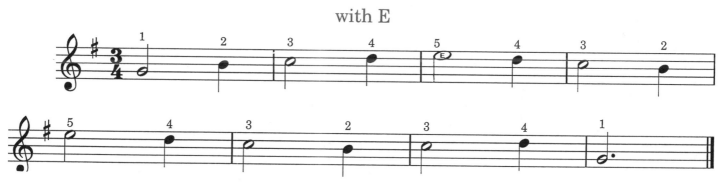

LEFT HAND AEROBICS
with E

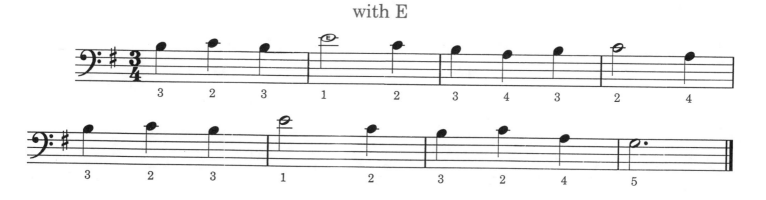

74

Place hands in G position.

LOVELY EVENING

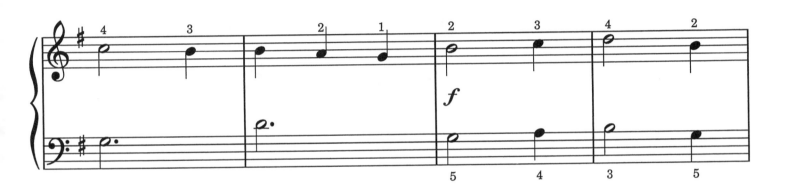

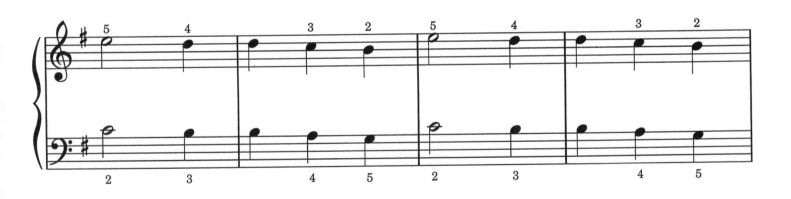

G

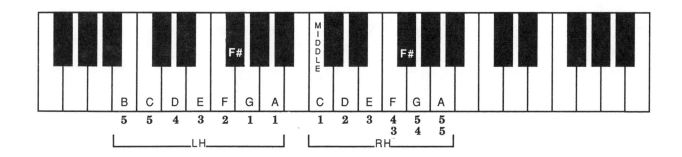

PEASANT DANCE

D. KABALEVSKY
arr. by S. Feldstein

Sturdily

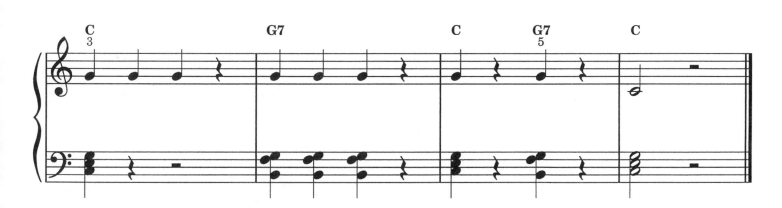

THEORY REVIEW

NOTES and CHORDS

Name the notes.

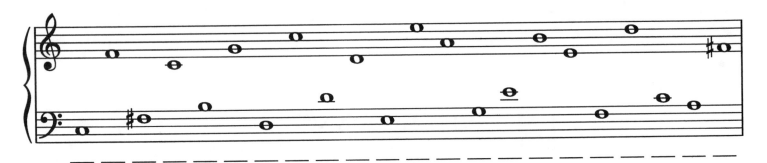

Write the letter names of the notes on the keyboard.

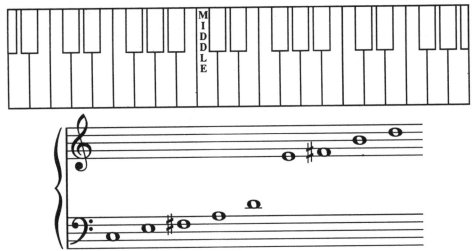

Name the chord.

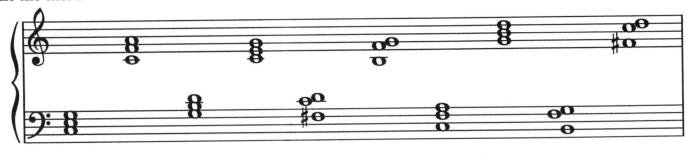

Draw the chord twice, once in the treble staff and once in the bass.

THE C CHORD
In A New Position

In the new position the C chord has the same notes as before (C E G)
   but positions them in a different order.

OLD POSITION NEW POSITION

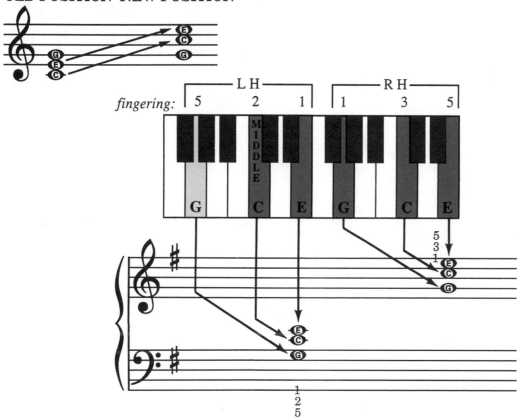

• Play the C chords with your LH.

• Play the C chords with your RH.

• Play the C chords with both hands.

78

COMBINING THE G, C and D⁷ CHORDS

- Place your fingers over the keyboard.
- Play the G chord with your LH.

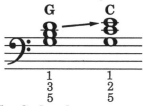

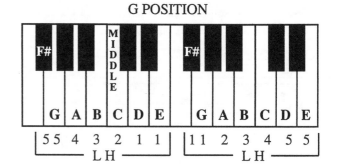

G POSITION

To play the C chord:
Finger 5 remains on G.
Finger 2 plays C.
Finger 1 moves up one key from D to E.

- Play the G, C, D⁷ chords with your LH.

- Play the G chord with your RH.

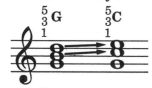

To play the C Chord:
Finger 1 remains on G.
Finger 3 moves up one key from B to C.
Finger 5 moves up one key from D to E.

- Play the G, C, D⁷ chords with your RH.

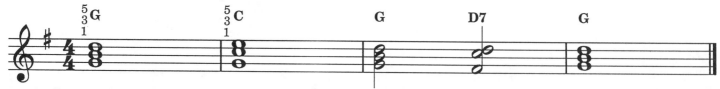

- Play the G, C, D⁷ chords with both hands.

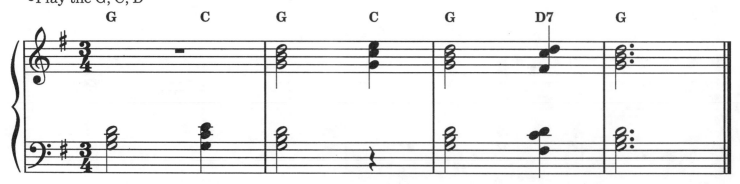

FRÉRE JACQUES
(Are You Sleeping?)

Frè - re Jac - ques, Frè - re Jac - ques, Dor - mez vous? Dor - mez vous?

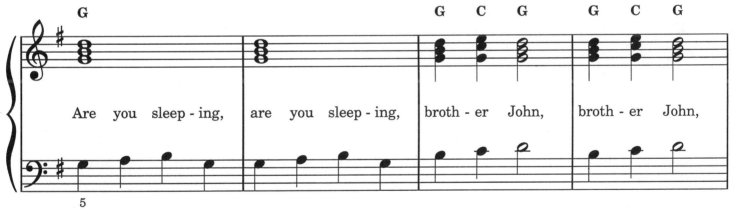

Son - nez les ma - ti - nes, son - nez les ma - ti - nes, Din - din, don, din - din don.

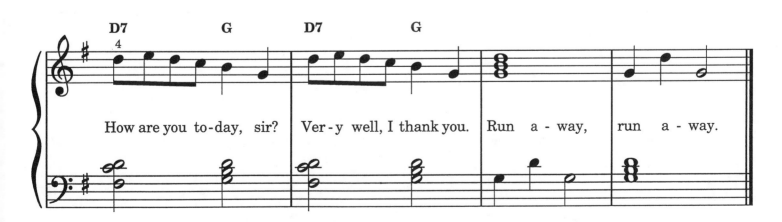

Are you sleep - ing, are you sleep - ing, broth - er John, broth - er John,

How are you to - day, sir? Ver - y well, I thank you. Run a - way, run a - way.

C MAJOR SCALE

The C MAJOR SCALE consists of the 8 white keys from C to C.

C SCALE POSITION

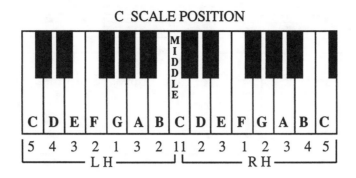

● Practice the following scale crossings.

RH - Ascending: the thumb goes under the 3rd finger when going from E to F.

RH - Descending: the third finger goes over the thumb when going from F to E.

LH - Ascending: the 3rd finger goes over the thumb when going from G to A.

LH - Descending: the thumb goes under the 3rd finger when going from A to G.

THEORY REVIEW
C MAJOR SCALE

The C Major Scale consists of the 8 white keys from C to C.

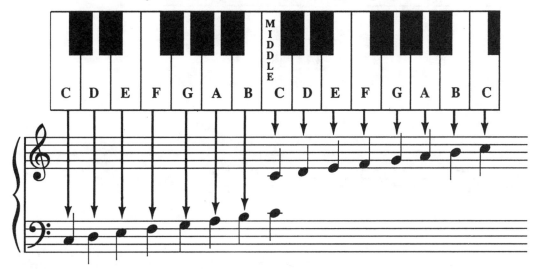

Draw the notes of the C scale from low to high.

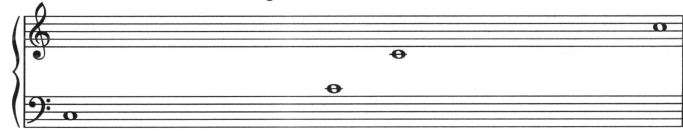

Draw the notes of the C scale from high to low.

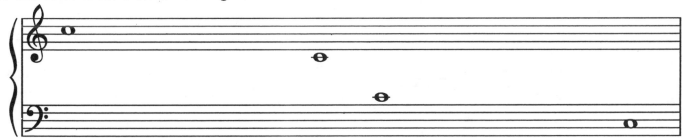

Indicate the fingering for the C scale in the treble staff.

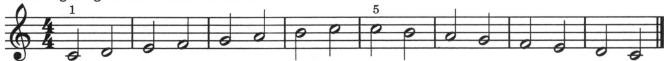

Indicate the fingering for the C scale in the bass staff.

A NEW RHYTHM

You already know that a dot adds one half the value of the original note.

A dotted quarter note 𝅘𝅥. equals 1 and 1/2 counts.

JOY TO THE WORLD

3rd finger over

MORE FAMILIAR MELODIES
USING DOTTED QUARTER AND EIGHTH NOTE

LONDON BRIDGE

Lon-don bridge is fall-ing down,

KUM-BA-YAH

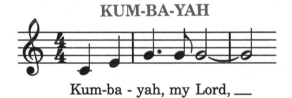

Kum-ba - yah, my Lord, ___

Place hands in C position.

MICHAEL, ROW THE BOAT ASHORE

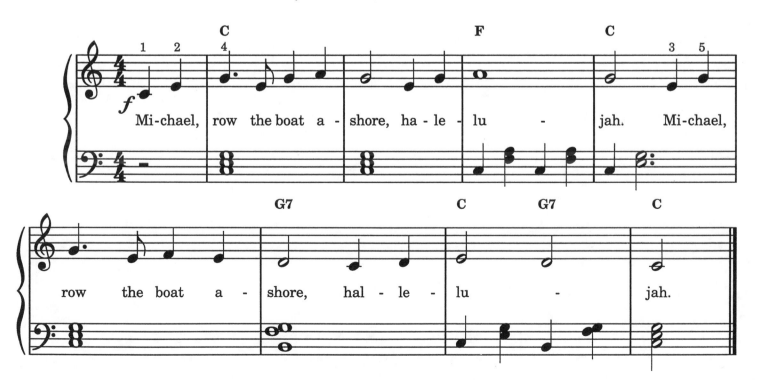

Mi-chael, row the boat a - shore, ha - le - lu - jah. Mi-chael, row the boat a - shore, hal - le - lu - jah.

Place LH in C position.

JOY TO THE WORLD

ISAAC WATTS
and
GEORGE F. HANDEL

Practice RH and LH alone, then together.

KUM-BA-YAH
G Position

SONATA
(Theme)

W.A. MOZART
arr. by S. Feldstein

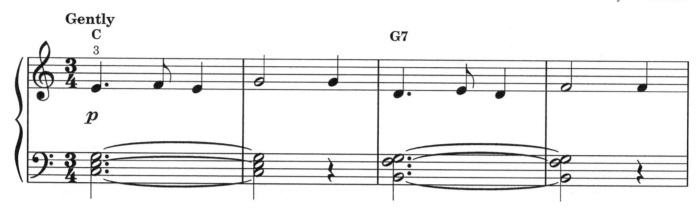

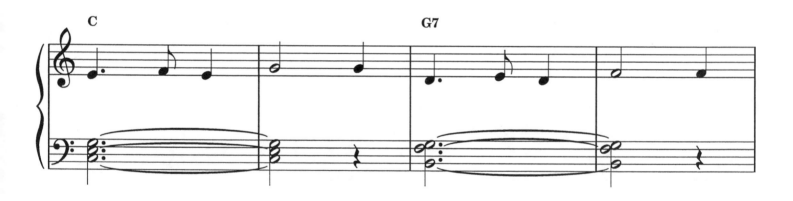

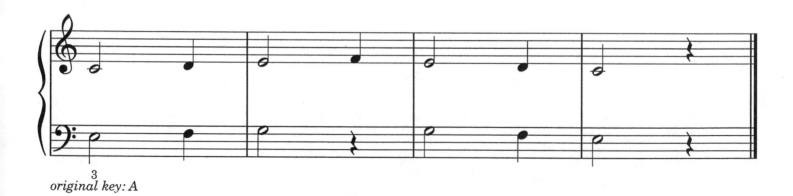

original key: A

Practice RH and LH alone, then together.
RH in G Position; LH in C Position

BLUE MOON

By LORENZ HART and
RICHARD RODGERS

THEORY REVIEW
DOTTED QUARTER NOTE

You already know that a dot adds one half the value of the original note.
A dotted quarter note (♩·) equals 1 and 1/2 counts.

♩ = one count (♫)   · = 1/2 count (♪)   ♩· = 1 and 1/2 counts (♫♪)

Write the beats under the notes indicated.

Add the bar lines in the appropriate places. End with a double bar.

Fill in the missing beats with either rests or notes.

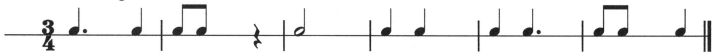

Draw the note that equals the number of beats.

♩ + ♪ = ♩·   ♩· + ♪ =

♫ + ♩ =   ♫ + ♪ + ♩· =

𝅗𝅥 + ♩ =   ♩· + ♪ + 𝅗𝅥 =

Add the beats of the notes indicated.

♩ + 𝅗𝅥 = **3**   ♩· + ♪ ♫ =

♩· + ♪ =   ♩· + ♪ + 𝅗𝅥 =

♩ + 𝅗𝅥· =   ♫ + ♩· + ♪ ♫ =

Add the bar lines and name the notes.

USING THE PEDALS

Most pianos have three pedals. The one on the right is called the DAMPER pedal. The one in the middle is the SOSTENUTO pedal and the one on the left is the SOFT pedal.*

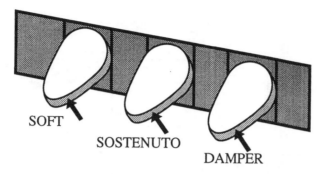

Now you can add the use of the damper pedal to your playing technique.
When depressed, the damper pedal allows the sound to ring . . . even after you have removed your finger from the key. Keep your right heel on the floor and depress the pedal with the ball of your foot. The pedal indication under the music tells you when to depress the pedal, when to lift up, and when to lift up and quickly depress again.

DOWN   UP/DOWN   UP

PEDAL WALTZ

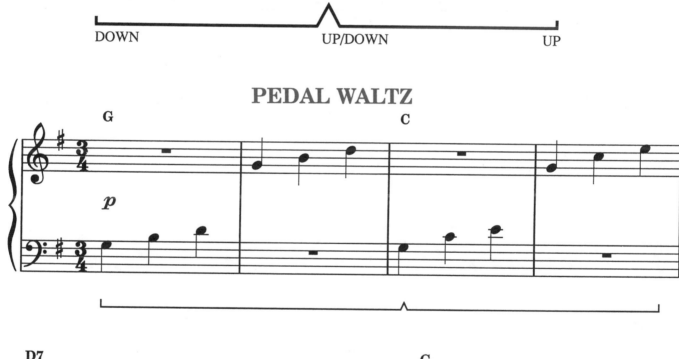

*Some pianos have only two pedals, the damper and the soft. Some electronic keyboards have only one pedal which can be assigned multiple functions.

BRIDAL CHORUS
from "Lohengrin"

R. WAGNER
arr. by S. Feldstein

Triumphantly

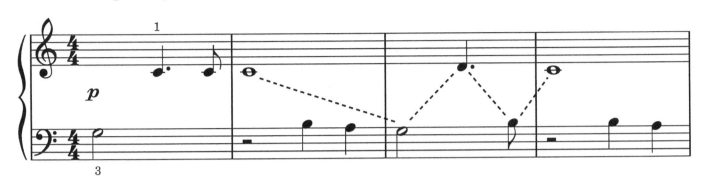

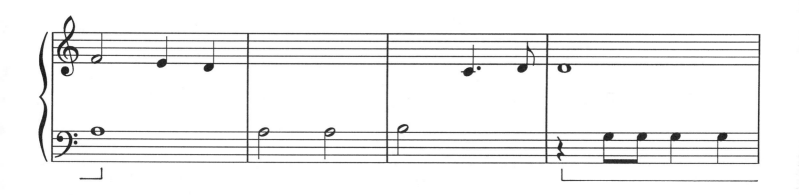

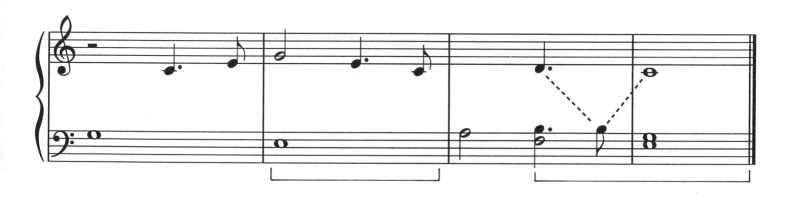

TECHNICAL ETUDE

C.L. HANON
arr. by S. Feldstein

Diligently

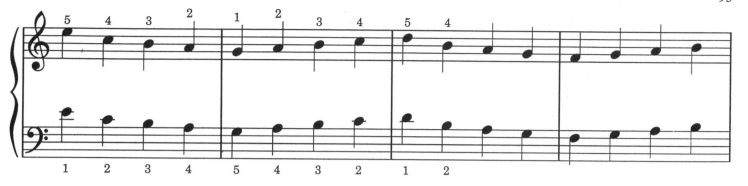

An ACCIDENTAL is a sharp (♯), flat (♭), or natural (♮) that does not occur in the key signature. Accidentals affect all following notes of that pitch within the measure.
A NATURAL (♮) cancels a sharp or flat.

OVER THE RAINBOW

Lyric by E.Y. HARBURG
Music by HAROLD ARLEN

* Play F sharp.
** Play F natural.

* To create an interesting effect play each note of the chord in quick succession from the bottom up. Your hands and the musical sound will have a rolling effect.